The Habit Loop: Unlocking the Power of Automatic Behavior Change

SaPH

CONTENTS

Do you struggle to make positive changes in your life, despite your best intentions? Have you ever wondered why some people seem to effortlessly stick to their healthy habits, while others struggle to stay on track? If so, "The Habit Loop: Unlocking the Power of Automatic Behavior Change" is the book for you!

Based on the latest research in habit formation and written by a leading expert in the field, this book provides a simple and actionable roadmap for developing lasting, automatic habits. By breaking down the habit formation process into four easy-to-follow steps, this book shows you how to create and sustain positive changes in your life, no matter how busy or overwhelmed you may feel.

Whether you want to exercise more, eat healthier, or improve your productivity, "The Habit Loop" offers practical tips and strategies for overcoming common obstacles and staying motivated on your journey towards habit formation. From setting clear goals to tracking your progress and celebrating your successes, this book provides all the tools you need to make lasting changes in your life.

But don't just take our word for it. "The Habit Loop" has received rave reviews from readers around the world, who have called it "a game-changer for habit formation" and "a must-read for anyone looking to make positive changes in their life." So why wait? Unlock the power of automatic behavior change today and start living the life you deserve!

CHAPTER 1: THE SCIENCE OF HABITS

Habits are automatic routines or behaviors that are triggered by certain cues or situations. They are often formed through repetition and reinforcement, and once they become ingrained in our daily lives, they can have a powerful impact on our behavior and decision-making.

Good habits can help us achieve our goals, improve our health and well-being, and make our lives more efficient and productive. For example, regular exercise or healthy eating habits can help us maintain physical fitness and prevent chronic diseases. Good study habits can help us succeed academically or professionally. Good financial habits can help us save money and achieve financial stability.

On the other hand, bad habits can be detrimental to our health, happiness, and success. For example, smoking, overeating, or excessive drinking can lead to serious health problems. Procrastination or lack of focus can negatively impact our productivity and success. Bad financial habits, such as overspending or failing to save money, can lead to financial instability and stress.

Habits are automatic routines or behaviors that are triggered by certain cues or situations. They are often formed through repetition and reinforcement, and once they become ingrained in our daily lives, they can have a powerful impact on our behavior and decision-making.

Good habits can help us achieve our goals, improve our health and well-being, and make our lives more efficient and productive. For example, regular exercise or healthy eating habits can help us maintain physical fitness and prevent chronic diseases. Good study habits can help us succeed academically or professionally. Good financial habits can help us save money and achieve financial stability.

On the other hand, bad habits can be detrimental to our health, happiness, and success. For example, smoking, overeating, or excessive drinking can lead to serious health problems. Procrastination or lack of focus can negatively impact our productivity and success. Bad financial habits, such as overspending or failing to save money, can lead to financial instability and stress.

Habits can be categorized into two types - good habits and bad habits. Good habits are those that have a positive impact on our lives, while bad habits have a negative impact. Understanding the difference between the two can help us make better choices and lead happier, healthier lives.

Examples of good habits include:

- ✓ Regular exercise or physical activity

- ✓ Eating a balanced and nutritious diet

- ✓ Getting enough sleep and rest

- ✓ Practicing stress-management techniques, such as meditation or deep breathing

- ✓ Saving money and managing finances responsibly

- ✓ Studying or learning something new every day

- ✓ Maintaining good hygiene and cleanliness habits

- ✓ Being punctual and reliable

These habits can have a positive impact on our physical and mental health, our relationships, and our overall well-being. For example, regular exercise can improve cardiovascular health, increase energy levels, and reduce stress and anxiety. Eating a balanced diet can improve digestion, boost immunity, and prevent chronic diseases.

On the other hand, examples of bad habits include:

- ✓ Smoking or using tobacco products

- ✓ Excessive drinking or drug use

- ✓ Overeating or indulging in unhealthy food choices

- ✓ Procrastination or lack of focus

- ✓ Overspending or failing to manage finances responsibly

- ✓ Neglecting personal hygiene or cleanliness

- ✓ Being dishonest or unreliable

These habits can have negative impacts on our health, relationships, and success. For example, smoking or using tobacco products can lead to serious health problems, such as lung cancer or heart disease. Overeating or indulging in unhealthy food choices can lead to obesity, diabetes, and other chronic conditions.

The habit loop is a three-part process that explains how habits are formed and sustained. It consists of a cue, a routine, and a reward.

> **Cue:** The cue is the trigger that initiates the habit. It can be anything from a time of day, a location, a person, an emotion, or any other environmental or internal factor that prompts the behavior.

Cues are critical to the formation and sustainability of habits. They act as signals that tell our brains to initiate a particular behavior. Once a habit has been formed, the cue becomes an automatic trigger that prompts the routine and, ultimately, the reward.

Cues can be internal or external. Internal cues are those that come from within us, such as an emotion, a thought, or a bodily sensation. External cues are those that come from our environment, such as a specific location or the presence of certain people or objects.

Cues can also be intentional or unintentional. Intentional cues are those that we actively seek out or create to prompt a behavior, such as setting an alarm to wake up early. Unintentional cues are those that we encounter naturally in our environment, such as the smell of fresh coffee in the morning that prompts us to make a cup.

Understanding the role of cues in the habit loop can help us to form new habits and break old ones. By identifying the cues that trigger our habits, we can modify or replace them to create a more positive outcome. For example, if someone wants to form a habit of drinking more water, they could set an intentional cue, such as leaving a water bottle on their desk or setting a reminder on their phone to drink water every hour.

➢ **Routine:** The routine is the actual behavior or action that the habit entails. It can be a physical action, a thought or emotion, or any other behavior that follows the cue.

Routines are the actions or behaviors that we perform automatically in response to a cue. They are the core of the habit loop, the behavior that we engage in without even thinking about it.

Routines can be positive or negative, depending on the habit. Positive routines are those that promote health, happiness, and productivity, while negative routines are those that have the opposite effect.

Routines can also be flexible or rigid. Flexible routines are those that can adapt to changes in the environment or situation, while rigid routines are those that cannot be easily changed or modified.

The routine is the most visible and tangible part of the habit loop, but it is also the most malleable. By changing the routine that follows a particular cue, we can alter our habits and create more positive behaviors.

For example, if someone wants to form a habit of exercising regularly, they could start with a simple routine such as doing a 10-minute workout every morning after waking up. As they become more comfortable with the routine, they can gradually increase the duration and intensity of the workout, making it a more permanent part of their daily routine.

> **Reward:** The reward is the positive outcome or result that reinforces the habit and encourages repetition. It can be anything from a feeling of satisfaction, a sense of accomplishment, or a physical reward such as a treat or a paycheck.

Rewards are the last part of the habit loop and are what reinforce the behavior and encourage repetition. Rewards can be immediate or delayed, tangible or intangible, and they can be positive or negative.

Positive rewards are those that increase the likelihood of a behavior being repeated, while negative rewards decrease the likelihood of a behavior being repeated.

Rewards are critical to habit formation because they help to cement the association between the cue and the routine. When we receive a reward after completing a routine, our brain releases dopamine, a chemical that is associated with pleasure and satisfaction. This dopamine release strengthens the connection between the cue and the routine, making it more likely that we will repeat the behavior in the future.

For example, if someone wants to form a habit of reading for 30 minutes every night before bed, they could reward themselves with a piece of chocolate or a few minutes of their favorite TV show after completing their reading routine. Over time, the reward of the chocolate or TV show becomes associated with the reading routine, making it more likely that the person will continue to read every night.

The habit loop is a powerful process that enables our brains to form automatic and efficient routines, which can be beneficial for tasks that require repetition and consistency. However, it can also be a double-edged sword, as it can lead to the formation of bad habits that are difficult to break.

For example, imagine someone who wants to start a habit of going to the gym every day. The cue could be getting home from work, the routine could be changing into workout clothes and driving to the gym, and the reward could be the endorphins and feeling of accomplishment after a workout. By repeating this habit loop every day, the person is more likely to sustain the habit and make it a permanent part of their routine.

On the other hand, imagine someone who has a bad habit of smoking. The cue could be a certain time of day or a social situation, the routine could be smoking a cigarette, and the reward could be the feeling of relaxation or stress relief. By repeating this habit loop every day, the person is more likely to continue smoking, even if they know it's bad for their health.

Understanding the habit loop and how it works can be a powerful tool for forming good habits and breaking bad ones. By identifying the cue, routine, and reward of a habit, we can modify or replace each part to create a more positive outcome and encourage healthier behaviors.

Here are some examples of how the habit loop applies to different types of habits:

Exercise:

✓ Cue: Time of day, gym location, workout clothes, or a workout buddy

✓ Routine: Exercise routine such as weight lifting, cardio, or yoga

✓ Reward: Feeling of accomplishment, endorphins from exercise, improved physical health

Diet:

✓ Cue: Time of day, mealtime, hunger, or a certain food trigger

✓ Routine: Eating habits such as portion control, avoiding certain foods, or meal prep

✓ Reward: Feeling of fullness or satisfaction, improved physical health, weight loss or maintenance

Productivity:

✓ Cue: Time of day, certain work environment, a specific task or project

✓ Routine: Work habits such as time management, prioritizing tasks, or taking breaks

✓ Reward: Feeling of accomplishment, recognition from others, improved work performance or efficiency

The habit loop can apply to many different types of habits and behaviors, as it is a fundamental part of how our brain learns and develops routines. By understanding how the habit loop works, individuals can identify their own cues, routines, and rewards and use that knowledge to create new, positive habits and break negative ones.

Identifying and analyzing the cues and rewards associated with your habits is a crucial step in understanding and changing your behavior. Here are some steps to help you do this:

Keeping a habit journal is a great way to track your habits and gain insight into your behavior. By writing down what you did, when you did it, and how you felt before and after, you can start to identify patterns and associations between your habits and your environment or emotions.

To start your habit journal, choose a notebook or a digital tool that you can easily access and use. Each day, write down the habits you want to track, along with the specific details mentioned above. Be as specific as possible and include any relevant details, such as the location, people involved, or specific emotions you experienced.

For example, if you want to track your eating habits, you might write down the following information:

Date: Monday, May 3 Time: 12:30 PM Location: Work cafeteria Habit: Eating lunch Routine: Salad with chicken, carrots, and cucumbers Cue: Feeling hungry after a morning meeting Reward: Feeling satisfied and energized for the rest of the afternoon

After a few days or weeks of tracking your habits, you can start to look for patterns and associations. For example, you might notice that you tend to snack on unhealthy foods when you feel stressed, or that you tend to skip workouts when you don't get enough sleep.

By identifying these patterns and associations, you can start to develop strategies to change your habits. For example, if you tend to snack when you're stressed, you might try taking a short walk or doing a quick meditation session instead. If you tend to skip workouts when you're tired, you might try going to bed earlier or adjusting your workout routine to a time of day when you have more energy.

After keeping a habit journal for some time, you can start to identify the cues or triggers that prompt your habits. These cues can be anything from a time of day, a location, a person, an emotion, or an activity that triggers the behavior.

To identify your cues, review your habit journal and look for patterns. Are there certain times of day when you tend to engage in a particular habit? Do you notice that you engage in the habit when you are in a particular location or around certain people? Are there particular emotions or activities that precede your habit?

As you review your journal, write down your cues and try to be as specific as possible. For example, if you notice that you tend to eat unhealthy snacks when you're feeling stressed at work, your cue might be "stressful work meetings" or "work-related stress." By identifying these cues, you can start to develop strategies to change your habits.

Once you've identified your cues, you can start to experiment with different strategies to change your behavior. For example, if you notice that you tend to snack on unhealthy foods when you're feeling stressed at work, you might try bringing healthy snacks to work or taking a short walk during your break to reduce your stress levels.

After identifying your cues, the next step in analyzing your habits is to look at the routine or behavior that follows the cue. This will help you understand the specific actions or behaviors that make up your habit.

To analyze your routine, start by reviewing your habit journal and identifying the specific actions or behaviors that you engage in after experiencing the cue. For example, if you tend to eat unhealthy snacks when you're feeling stressed at work, your routine might include walking to the vending machine, selecting a snack, and eating it at your desk.

Once you have identified the routine, write down the specific actions or behaviors and be as detailed as possible. For example, you might write down "Walk to the vending machine," "Select a bag of chips," "Pay for the snack," and "Eat the chips at my desk." By breaking down the routine into specific actions, you can start to see where you might be able to make changes.

Analyzing your routine can help you identify specific areas where you can make changes to your habits. For example, if you want to stop snacking on unhealthy foods at work, you might try bringing healthy snacks to work or finding a different way to manage your stress levels.

After analyzing your routine, the next step in understanding your habits is to identify the rewards or positive outcomes that follow. Rewards are what reinforce the behavior and encourage you to repeat it in the future. By identifying the rewards associated with your habits, you can start to understand why you engage in certain behaviors and develop strategies to create new, positive habits.

To identify your rewards, review your habit journal and ask yourself what you gain from completing the behavior. Is it a feeling of accomplishment, satisfaction, or a tangible reward such as food or money? Be honest with yourself and try to identify the specific reward that motivates you to engage in the behavior.

For example, if you tend to procrastinate by checking social media, your reward might be the temporary distraction and entertainment provided by the app. If you tend to exercise regularly, your reward might be the feeling of accomplishment and satisfaction that comes from completing a workout.

Once you have identified your rewards, write them down and try to be as specific as possible. For example, you might write down "Temporary distraction and entertainment," "Feeling of accomplishment and satisfaction," or "Tangible reward such as food or money."

When you experiment with new routines and rewards, it's important to be patient and persistent. It takes time and repetition for a new habit to form, so don't expect immediate results. You may also need to adjust your routine or reward if you find that it's not working for you.

Another strategy is to gradually increase the difficulty of the routine over time. For example, if you want to form a habit of running, start with a short distance and gradually increase it as your fitness level improves. This helps prevent burnout and makes the habit more sustainable in the long term.

Remember that forming new habits is a process, and it's okay to make mistakes along the way. Don't beat yourself up if you slip up or miss a day, just get back on track and keep going. With time and practice, you can transform your habits and unlock the power of automatic behavior change.

Dopamine is a neurotransmitter that plays a crucial role in our brain's reward system. It is often associated with pleasure and positive reinforcement, which makes it a key player in the formation of habits. When we engage in a behavior that we find pleasurable or rewarding, such as eating our favorite food or receiving positive feedback, our brain releases dopamine, creating a feeling of pleasure and reinforcing the behavior.

Over time, the release of dopamine associated with the behavior creates a habit loop, making it easier and more automatic to engage in the behavior. This is why habits can be difficult to break, as our brain has become wired to associate the behavior with a positive outcome. Understanding the role of dopamine in habit formation can help us identify and change our habits, as we can learn to create new habits that provide a similar level of dopamine release while eliminating the negative effects of our old habits.

Dopamine plays a crucial role in reinforcing the habit loop and encouraging the repetition of habits. When we experience a cue that prompts a behavior, our brain releases dopamine in anticipation of the reward that will follow. This release of dopamine creates a positive feeling that motivates us to perform the routine or behavior in order to receive the reward.

Over time, our brain becomes conditioned to associate the cue and routine with the reward, creating a strong neural pathway that reinforces the habit loop. The more we repeat the habit, the stronger this neural pathway becomes, making it easier and more automatic for us to perform the habit in the future.

However, this process can also be a double-edged sword. Habits that release high levels of dopamine, such as those related to drug or alcohol addiction, can lead to compulsive behaviors and a loss of control. By understanding the role of dopamine in habit formation, we can take steps to develop healthy habits and avoid the negative effects of addictive behaviors.

While dopamine plays an important role in forming habits, it can also have potential downsides if its effects are not properly managed. Dopamine can reinforce the habit loop and encourage repetition of habits, but it can also lead to addiction or compulsive behavior if the habits are negative or harmful.

For example, someone who becomes addicted to drugs or alcohol may experience a surge of dopamine in response to the cue or trigger associated with substance use. Over time, the individual's brain begins to associate the cue and routine with the reward of dopamine release, leading to compulsive drug-seeking behavior that can be difficult to break.

Similarly, someone who becomes addicted to video games may experience a surge of dopamine in response to the cue of starting up a game, and the routine of playing and achieving small rewards or accomplishments within the game. This can lead to compulsive gaming behavior that interferes with other aspects of the person's life.

It is important to recognize the potential downsides of dopamine-related habit formation and take steps to manage the effects of dopamine on our behavior. This can include setting limits on our exposure to certain cues, finding healthy and positive rewards to reinforce our habits, and seeking help if we feel that our habits are becoming compulsive or addictive.

CHAPTER 2: THE FOUR STEPS TO AUTOMATIC HABITS

In order to create a new habit, it's important to have a systematic approach that includes identifying your cue, designing your routine, choosing your reward, and making it automatic. The four steps to automatic habits are a practical and effective framework that can help you develop long-lasting habits that are beneficial for your personal and professional life.

The Importance of having a systematic approach to habit formation:

Without a systematic approach to habit formation, it's easy to become overwhelmed and give up on your efforts to create new habits. The four steps provide a clear roadmap to follow, which makes it easier to stay on track and achieve your goals. By following a systematic approach, you'll also be able to identify and address any obstacles that may arise along the way, and adjust your approach accordingly.

The four steps to automatic habits can be applied to any habit you want to develop, whether it's related to health and fitness, personal growth, or productivity. By following this framework, you can make habit formation an automatic and effortless part of your daily routine, which can lead to significant improvements in your life over time.

Following the four-step process can bring numerous benefits to your habit-forming journey. By breaking down the process of habit formation into specific steps, you can approach it in a more systematic and intentional way. Here are some benefits of following the four-step process:

> **Clarity:** The four-step process provides a clear framework for developing new habits. By breaking down the process into distinct steps, you can focus on each element of the habit loop and develop a deeper understanding of how it works.

> **Focus:** The process helps you to identify and focus on the specific cues, routines, and rewards that are associated with your desired habit. This helps you to be more

intentional about your behavior and ensures that you are targeting the right aspects of your habit loop.

> **Flexibility:** The process is flexible enough to be applied to any habit you want to form, whether it's related to your health, productivity, relationships, or any other area of your life. This means that you can use the same process to form any habit you want, and customize it to fit your individual needs.

> **Increased likelihood of success:** By following a systematic approach, you increase your chances of success in forming new habits. The process helps you to be more intentional and focused, and to make small, incremental changes that are more sustainable in the long run.

Step 1 of the four-step process to automatic habits is identifying your cue. This step is critical to the habit formation process because it helps you recognize the triggers that prompt your behavior. Without identifying your cues, it can be difficult to break bad habits or create new ones.

The cue can be anything that prompts your behavior, such as a specific time of day, a particular location, a particular emotion, or even the presence of certain people. For example, if you have a habit of eating junk food after work, your cue might be arriving home or feeling stressed after a long day at work.

By identifying your cue, you can take steps to either avoid or modify the trigger that prompts your behavior. This will help you break bad habits and replace them with new, healthier habits.

There are several techniques you can use to identify your cues for a particular habit. Here are some examples:

> **Keep a habit journal:** As mentioned earlier, keeping a journal is a great way to track your habits and identify your cues. Write down the habit you want to form, and then record when and where you perform it, as well as any

emotions or environmental factors that may have contributed to the behavior.

➢ **Self-reflection exercises:** Take some time to reflect on your behavior and identify any triggers or patterns. Ask yourself questions such as "What usually happens right before I engage in this behavior?" or "What emotion am I feeling when I engage in this behavior?" This can help you identify the cue that is prompting your behavior.

➢ **Experimentation:** Sometimes it may be difficult to identify your cues through self-reflection or journaling alone. In this case, you may need to experiment with different cues to see what works. For example, if you're trying to form a habit of exercising in the morning but aren't sure what your cue is, try different cues such as setting an alarm, leaving your workout clothes out, or drinking a glass of water first thing in the morning. Pay attention to which cues make it easier for you to engage in the behavior.

Common cues can be anything from a specific time of day, location, or feeling, to an action or event that prompts a certain behavior. Here are some examples of common cues and how to use them to trigger desired behaviors:

➢ **Time of day:** If you want to form a habit of reading before bed, use the time of day as a cue. Set a specific time, such as 9 pm, as your reading time, and make sure to stick to it every day.

➢ **Location:** If you want to form a habit of exercising, use a specific location as your cue. For example, make it a habit to go to the gym every morning before work, or take a walk around your neighborhood after dinner.

➢ **Feeling:** If you want to form a habit of meditation or deep breathing, use a feeling as your cue. When you start to feel stressed or anxious, take a few minutes to practice your breathing or meditation.

> **Action:** If you want to form a habit of flossing your teeth every day, use a specific action as your cue. For example, make it a habit to floss your teeth right after you brush them.

By using specific cues to trigger desired behaviors, you can create a strong habit loop that makes it easier to stick to your habits over time.

Step 2 of the Four Steps to Automatic Habits is designing your routine. Once you have identified your cue, the next step is to create a routine or behavior that will follow the cue. It is important to create a routine that is specific and achievable, meaning that it is realistic and can be consistently executed.

Designing a routine is important because it helps create structure and consistency in your habits. Having a routine makes it easier for your brain to follow the habit loop and reinforces the behavior you want to establish. A specific routine also helps you avoid decision fatigue and saves mental energy, making it easier to stick to the habit.

To design your routine, start by thinking about the behavior you want to establish and breaking it down into small, achievable steps. For example, if you want to establish a habit of exercising in the morning, your routine might include the following steps: wake up at a specific time, put on workout clothes, drink a glass of water, stretch, and then begin your workout. By breaking down the behavior into specific steps, you can create a routine that is achievable and easy to follow.

It is also important to make your routine enjoyable or rewarding in some way. This can help reinforce the behavior and make it more automatic. For example, if you want to establish a habit of reading before bed, you might create a routine of dimming the lights, brewing a cup of tea, and then settling down with a good book. By making the routine enjoyable, you are more likely to stick to the behavior and form a habit.

When it comes to designing your routine, there are a few tips to keep in mind to ensure that it is specific, achievable, and tailored to your needs. Here are some tips:

➤ **Break it down into small steps:** Rather than trying to tackle a complex behavior all at once, break it down into smaller, more manageable steps. This will help you avoid feeling overwhelmed and make it easier to stick with the routine over time. For example, if your goal is to start running every morning, start by committing to a short walk each morning, and then gradually increase your distance and intensity over time.

➤ **Make it fit into your schedule:** To make your routine sustainable, make sure it fits into your schedule and is something you can realistically commit to on a daily basis. Consider the time of day that works best for you and the amount of time you have available, and design your routine accordingly.

➤ **Keep it simple:** A simple routine is more likely to be successful than a complicated one. Focus on one specific behavior or action and design your routine around that. For example, if your goal is to start meditating every day, start with a simple routine of just five minutes per day, and then gradually increase your time as you become more comfortable with the practice.

➤ **Visualize yourself doing it:** Spend some time visualizing yourself completing your routine successfully. This can help build confidence and increase motivation, making it easier to stick with the habit over time.

By following these tips, you can design a routine that is specific, achievable, and tailored to your needs, making it more likely that you will be able to successfully form a new habit.

Here are some examples of effective routines for common habits:

➢ **Exercise:** Start with a warm-up, such as light cardio or stretching, followed by a series of exercises targeting different muscle groups. Set a specific goal, such as a certain number of reps or sets, and gradually increase the difficulty as you improve. Finish with a cool-down and stretching to prevent injury.

➢ **Meditation:** Find a quiet and comfortable place to sit or lie down. Set a specific time limit, such as 5 or 10 minutes, and focus on your breath or a specific mantra. When your mind wanders, gently bring it back to your breath or mantra. Consistency is key, so try to meditate at the same time and place every day.

➢ **Healthy Eating:** Plan your meals in advance, including a variety of nutrient-dense foods such as fruits, vegetables, lean proteins, and whole grains. Make sure to incorporate snacks and avoid skipping meals to maintain steady blood sugar levels. Consider tracking your food intake to ensure you are meeting your nutritional goals.

➢ **Reading:** Set aside a specific time each day for reading, such as before bed or during your lunch break. Choose a book that interests you and set a goal for how many pages or chapters you want to read each day. Minimize distractions and make reading a priority during your designated time.

Remember, everyone's routine will be different based on their individual goals and lifestyle. It's important to find a routine that works for you and is sustainable over the long-term.

The third step in creating automatic habits is choosing a reward that is meaningful and motivating. Rewards help reinforce the habit loop by providing positive feedback to the brain and increasing the likelihood of habit formation. Choosing the right reward is important because it can make the difference between sticking with the habit or giving up.

One important aspect of choosing a reward is to make sure it is meaningful to you personally. This means that the reward should be something that you genuinely enjoy or find satisfying. For example, if your goal is to exercise regularly, rewarding yourself with a piece of cake might not be the best option if you are trying to improve your diet. Instead, consider rewarding yourself with a relaxing bubble bath or some extra time to read your favorite book.

Another important consideration when choosing a reward is to make sure it is motivating enough to keep you interested in the habit. For example, if your goal is to wake up earlier to have more time for work or hobbies, you might reward yourself with a delicious cup of coffee or a special breakfast. This can make waking up early more appealing and enjoyable.

It is also important to choose a reward that is appropriate for the habit you are trying to form. For example, if your goal is to save money, spending money on a reward might not be the best option. Instead, consider rewarding yourself with something free or low-cost, such as a relaxing evening at home or a special treat you have been saving in the pantry.

Here are some tips for choosing a reward that aligns with your values and goals:

> **Identify what motivates you:** Think about what you enjoy or what you find fulfilling. If you're trying to develop a habit of exercise, a reward that you enjoy, such as watching your favorite show, may be motivating for you.

> **Consider long-term rewards:** While immediate rewards, such as a piece of candy, can be satisfying, they may not be sustainable in the long run. Instead, consider choosing a reward that aligns with your long-term goals, such as a healthy meal or an item you've been saving up for.

> **Connect the reward to the habit:** The reward should be

directly related to the habit you're trying to form. For example, if you're trying to develop a habit of reading, your reward could be buying a new book.

➤ **Make the reward consistent:** Consistency is key when it comes to developing habits, and the same is true for rewards. If you consistently reward yourself for completing the habit, it will reinforce the behavior and make it more likely to stick.

➤ **Mix it up:** While consistency is important, it's also important to mix up your rewards from time to time. This will keep things interesting and prevent you from getting bored with the habit.

Here are some examples of effective rewards for different types of habits:

➤ **Exercise:** A hot shower, a healthy snack, listening to music, or watching an episode of your favorite show.

➤ **Healthy eating:** Trying a new healthy recipe, buying a new kitchen gadget or tool, going out to a healthy restaurant, or treating yourself to a healthy dessert.

➤ **Productivity:** Taking a break to do something you enjoy, such as reading or listening to music, treating yourself to a coffee or tea, or spending time with friends or family.

➤ **Meditation or mindfulness:** Relaxing in a quiet space, enjoying a hot drink, taking a walk in nature, or listening to calming music.

➤ **Reading:** Treating yourself to a new book, spending time in a cozy reading spot, or enjoying a special beverage or snack while you read.

Remember, the key to choosing an effective reward is to make sure it is something that is motivating and aligns with your values and goals.

Making a habit automatic requires consistent repetition over time. When a behavior is repeated enough times, it becomes second nature and requires minimal effort or thought. This is why **Step 4** is crucial in the habit-forming process.

Repetition is necessary to strengthen the neural pathways in the brain associated with the habit loop. Every time a behavior is repeated, the connection between the cue, routine, and reward becomes stronger. This is because the release of dopamine reinforces the behavior and encourages its repetition.

Consistency is also important in making a habit automatic. If the behavior is only performed occasionally, the brain does not receive enough reinforcement to make it automatic. Therefore, it is important to set a specific time and place for the behavior to occur consistently. For example, if you want to form a habit of reading before bed, set aside a specific time each night to do so.

Making a habit automatic also requires patience and persistence. It can take anywhere from a few weeks to several months for a behavior to become automatic, depending on the complexity of the habit and the individual. It is important to not get discouraged if progress is slow, and to continue repeating the behavior consistently.

Ultimately, the goal of making a habit automatic is to create a behavior that requires little to no conscious effort, allowing more mental energy to be focused on other tasks and goals.

There are several techniques that can help reinforce a habit and make it automatic. Here are a few:

> ➤ Use visual cues: Place reminders in visible places to serve as cues for your habit. For example, if you want to form a habit of drinking more water, place a water bottle on your

desk or carry a reusable water bottle with you.

Visual cues can be very helpful in making habits more automatic. Here are some additional examples of using visual cues:

If you want to form a habit of flossing your teeth, place the floss in a visible spot next to your toothbrush as a reminder to do it.

If you want to form a habit of reading before bed, leave the book you want to read on your nightstand.

If you want to form a habit of taking vitamins or medication, place them in a spot where you will see them every day, such as on your kitchen counter or next to your toothbrush.

By placing visual cues in strategic locations, you can help remind yourself to perform the habit until it becomes more automatic.

➢ Setting reminders can be a useful technique to help reinforce a habit and ensure consistency. There are several ways to set reminders, depending on your preference and lifestyle. Here are some examples:

Alarms: You can set alarms on your phone or other devices to remind you to complete your habit at a specific time. For example, if you want to form a habit of taking a daily walk at 3 pm, set an alarm on your phone to remind you.

Calendar reminders: If you use a digital calendar, you can create reminders that will pop up on your screen at specific times. For example, if you want to form a habit of meditating in the morning, you can set a reminder on your calendar to do so at 7 am.

Habit-tracking apps: There are several apps available that can help you track your habits and send reminders to complete them. These apps can also provide motivation and encouragement by tracking your progress and providing rewards or incentives.

Sticky notes: You can place sticky notes around your home or workspace to serve as visual reminders of your habit. For example, if you want to form a habit of drinking more water, place a sticky note on your fridge or water bottle to remind you to drink water throughout the day.

By setting reminders, you are creating triggers that will help reinforce your habit and make it more automatic over time.

Habit stacking is a powerful technique to help make a new habit automatic. By combining the new habit with an existing habit, you create a trigger that helps reinforce the new behavior. This technique works because the existing habit is already ingrained in your brain, so it's easier to add a new behavior onto it.

To use habit stacking, identify an existing habit that you do consistently and pair it with your new habit. For example, if you want to start a habit of reading before bed, you could stack it with your existing habit of getting into bed. So, every night after you get into bed, you spend 10 minutes reading. Another example is if you want to start a habit of taking your vitamins, you could stack it with your existing habit of drinking your morning coffee. So, every morning after you drink your coffee, you take your vitamins.

The key is to choose an existing habit that you do every day without fail and to make sure the new habit is something that can be done immediately after the existing habit. With habit stacking, you can easily integrate new habits into your daily routine and make them automatic.

Positive affirmations can be a powerful tool in creating and reinforcing habits. Affirmations are positive statements that can help to shift your mindset and beliefs, and they can be used to reinforce your commitment to your habit.

To use positive affirmations, start by identifying a few key phrases that resonate with you and align with your habit goals. These phrases should be positive, present-tense statements that reflect the habits you want to create.

For example, if you want to form a habit of practicing gratitude, you could use affirmations like:

✓ I am grateful for all the blessings in my life

✓ Every day, I find new things to be grateful for

✓ Gratitude comes naturally to me

Repeat your affirmations to yourself throughout the day, especially when you're feeling unmotivated or discouraged. You can also write them down and display them in a visible place, such as on your mirror or computer monitor.

By using positive affirmations, you can shift your mindset and beliefs to support your habit goals, making it easier to stick to your new habits and create lasting change.

Making your habit convenient can be a powerful technique for ensuring that you consistently follow through with your routine. By removing any obstacles or barriers that might get in the way, you can make it easier to complete your habit and increase the likelihood of making it automatic.

There are many ways to make a habit convenient, depending on the specific habit and your individual circumstances. Here are some examples:

➢ **Prepare in advance:** Make preparations for your habit in advance to save time and effort. For example, if you want to start a habit of cooking healthy meals, you could prepare your ingredients and plan your meals for the week in advance.

> **Simplify your environment:** Create an environment that supports your habit by removing any distractions or obstacles. For example, if you want to form a habit of meditating, create a peaceful and clutter-free space in your home where you can meditate without any interruptions.

> **Use technology:** Use technology to make your habit more convenient. For example, if you want to form a habit of tracking your daily water intake, use an app or smart water bottle that automatically tracks your progress.

> **Make it portable:** If your habit is something that can be done on the go, make it portable. For example, if you want to form a habit of practicing yoga, find a yoga mat that is lightweight and easy to carry with you.

Overcoming obstacles and staying motivated are key factors in developing and maintaining a new habit. Here are some tips for staying on track:

> **Plan for obstacles:** Anticipate potential barriers and plan ahead for how you will overcome them. For example, if you want to exercise in the morning but struggle with waking up early, plan to set your alarm clock earlier and have your workout clothes ready to go.

> **Track your progress:** Use a habit-tracking app or a journal to keep track of your progress. Seeing your progress can be motivating and help you stay on track.

> **Get an accountability partner:** Find a friend or family member who can help keep you accountable and provide support when you need it.

> **Celebrate small wins:** Celebrate small milestones and

accomplishments along the way. This can help boost motivation and reinforce the habit.

➤ **Be kind to yourself:** Don't be too hard on yourself if you miss a day or struggle with the habit at first. Remember that developing a new habit takes time and effort, and it's okay to make mistakes along the way.

Bringing the four steps of identifying the cue, designing the routine, choosing the reward, and making it automatic together into a cohesive strategy can help to create a successful habit-forming plan. Here are some tips for putting the steps together:

➤ **Start with a clear goal:** Before beginning to identify cues or design routines, start with a clear and specific goal. This can help to ensure that each step is working towards the same outcome.

➤ **Be flexible:** It's important to remember that habit formation is not a one-size-fits-all process. Be open to adjusting and experimenting with the steps to find what works best for you.

➤ **Track your progress:** Use a habit-tracking app or journal to track your progress and hold yourself accountable. This can also help you to identify patterns or areas that need improvement.

➤ **Celebrate your successes:** Celebrate when you achieve your goal or reach a milestone in your habit-forming journey. This can help to reinforce the habit and keep you motivated.

➤ **Don't give up:** Remember that forming a habit takes time and consistency. Don't give up if you miss a day or struggle with the routine. Keep going and focus on progress, not perfection.

Here are some examples of successful habit formation using the four-step process:

> **Exercise:** A person wants to form a habit of exercising in the morning. They identify their cue as waking up and design a routine that involves stretching, going for a run, and taking a shower. Their chosen reward is a healthy breakfast and a sense of accomplishment. To make the habit automatic, they set reminders on their phone and place their running shoes and workout clothes in a visible place.

> **Meditation:** A person wants to form a habit of meditating every day. They identify their cue as finishing their morning coffee and design a routine that involves finding a quiet spot, sitting in a comfortable position, and focusing on their breath for 10 minutes. Their chosen reward is a feeling of calm and centeredness. To make the habit automatic, they use a guided meditation app and set a reminder on their phone.

> **Reading:** A person wants to form a habit of reading more. They identify their cue as finishing dinner and design a routine that involves choosing a book, setting a timer for 30 minutes, and reading in a comfortable spot. Their chosen reward is a feeling of relaxation and enjoyment. To make the habit automatic, they keep a book on their bedside table and use a reading log to track their progress.

These examples show how the four-step process can be applied to different habits and tailored to individual preferences and lifestyles. By following a systematic approach, it is possible to create new habits that stick and contribute to a healthier and happier life.

When trying to form a new habit using the four-step process, there are a few common pitfalls to avoid. By being aware of these pitfalls, you can troubleshoot and overcome them to stay on track with your habit-forming goals. Here are some tips to help you troubleshoot common challenges:

> **Not starting small enough:** It's important to break down your routine into small, manageable steps. If you try to tackle too much too soon, you may become overwhelmed and give up. Start with a small, achievable goal and build on it over time.

> **Losing motivation:** It's normal to experience a dip in motivation at some point during the habit-forming process. To stay motivated, remind yourself of why you started in the first place, visualize the benefits of the habit, and use positive affirmations to stay focused on your goal.

> **Being too hard on yourself:** It's easy to get discouraged when you slip up or miss a day of your habit. Instead of beating yourself up, be compassionate and recognize that forming a new habit takes time and effort. If you fall off track, simply pick yourself up and start again.

> **Allowing exceptions:** While it's important to be flexible and forgiving, it's also important to hold yourself accountable. Don't allow exceptions to your habit without a good reason. If you make an exception, make sure it's a conscious choice rather than a slip-up.

> **Not tracking progress:** It can be helpful to track your progress over time to see how far you've come and to stay motivated. Use a habit-tracking app, journal, or calendar to mark off each day that you complete your habit.

In conclusion, the four-step process of identifying cues, designing a routine, choosing a reward, and making it automatic is a powerful tool for forming automatic habits. By following this process, you can create new, positive habits that align with your goals and values. It's important to be patient and consistent when forming new habits, as it takes time for them to become automatic. Remember to celebrate small victories along the way and to learn from any setbacks.

By applying these four steps, you can create a habit-forming strategy that is tailored to your unique needs and goals. With dedication and perseverance, you can overcome common pitfalls and troubleshoot any obstacles that arise. Ultimately, the goal is to create positive habits that become a natural part of your daily routine, leading to a happier, healthier, and more fulfilling life. So go ahead, start applying the four steps today and see how they can transform your habits and your life.

CHAPTER 3: SETTING GOALS AND MEASURING PROGRESS

Setting goals and tracking progress is an essential part of achieving success in any area of life. Whether you are looking to improve your health, build a career, or learn a new skill, setting clear and measurable goals can help you stay focused and motivated. In this chapter, we will explore the importance of setting goals and measuring progress, as well as techniques for effective goal-setting and tracking.

Setting goals is important for several reasons. First, it provides clarity on what you want to achieve, which can help you stay focused and motivated. When you have a clear idea of what you want to accomplish, it is easier to create a plan of action and work towards achieving your goals. Additionally, setting goals helps to measure progress and track your success. It allows you to celebrate your accomplishments and identify areas where you need to improve. Finally, setting goals can boost your self-confidence and self-esteem, as you prove to yourself that you are capable of achieving what you set out to do.

Not setting goals can lead to a lack of direction and purpose in life. It may result in feeling like you are drifting through life without a clear sense of what you want to achieve. Without goals, it can be difficult to measure progress and determine whether you are making meaningful advancements in your personal or professional life. Additionally, without goals, it may be challenging to identify priorities, and as a result, you may find yourself getting sidetracked by tasks that are not essential to your growth or development. Ultimately, the absence of clear goals can hinder your ability to reach your full potential and may leave you feeling unfulfilled.

SMART goals are an effective way to set goals that are specific, measurable, achievable, relevant, and time-bound. The SMART goal framework can help you create goals that are well-defined and actionable, which can increase your chances of success.

Here's a breakdown of each component of a SMART goal:

> **Specific:** Goals should be clear and concise. Rather than

setting a general goal like "lose weight," try to be more specific, such as "lose 10 pounds in the next 3 months."

➤ **Measurable:** Goals should have a way of measuring progress. This helps to ensure that you stay on track and can track your progress along the way. For example, if your goal is to read more, you might set a measurable goal of reading for 30 minutes every day.

➤ **Achievable:** Goals should be realistic and achievable. This means taking into account your current situation and resources, and setting goals that are challenging but within reach. For example, if you want to learn a new language, it's important to set a goal that is challenging but achievable based on your current level of proficiency.

➤ **Relevant:** Goals should be relevant to your overall aspirations and desires. This means setting goals that align with your values and priorities. For example, if you value physical health, setting a goal to exercise regularly would be relevant.

➤ **Time-bound:** Goals should have a specific deadline for completion. This helps to create a sense of urgency and accountability, and allows you to measure progress over time. For example, if you want to start a new business, setting a goal to launch your product by a specific date creates a sense of urgency and helps you stay focused.

By setting SMART goals, you can create a clear and actionable plan for achieving your desired outcome. It helps you to break down larger goals into smaller, more manageable tasks, and provides a framework for tracking progress along the way.

Breaking down long-term goals into smaller, achievable steps is an important technique for effective goal-setting. This allows you to focus on what you can do in the present to make progress towards your long-term goal. Here are some tips for breaking down long-term goals:

> **Define your long-term goal:** Start by defining your long-term goal. This should be a specific, measurable, and realistic goal that you want to achieve within a certain timeframe.

> **Identify the milestones:** Break down your long-term goal into smaller, achievable milestones. These milestones should be specific and measurable, and they should represent significant progress towards your long-term goal.

> **Create an action plan:** Once you have identified your milestones, create an action plan for each one. This plan should include specific steps that you can take to achieve each milestone.

> **Prioritize your actions:** Prioritize the actions that you need to take to achieve each milestone. Focus on the actions that are most important and that will have the biggest impact on your progress.

> **Set deadlines:** Set deadlines for each milestone and for each action step within your action plan. This will help you stay on track and ensure that you are making progress towards your long-term goal.

> **Monitor your progress:** Regularly monitor your progress towards each milestone. This will help you stay motivated and make adjustments to your action plan as needed.

Breaking down long-term goals into smaller, achievable steps can make it easier to stay motivated and make progress towards your goals. By focusing on the steps that you can take in the present, you can build momentum and make steady progress towards your long-term goal.

Writing down your goals can be a powerful tool in achieving them. When you write down your goals, you make them more concrete and tangible, which can help you stay focused and motivated. Here are some of the benefits of writing down your goals:

> **Clarity:** Writing down your goals helps you clarify exactly what it is you want to achieve. It forces you to think about your goals in concrete terms, which can help you identify any gaps or inconsistencies in your thinking.

> **Focus:** Writing down your goals helps you stay focused on what you want to achieve. When you have a clear, written record of your goals, you can easily remind yourself of what you're working towards, which can help you stay motivated.

> **Accountability:** Writing down your goals can help you hold yourself accountable for achieving them. When you write down your goals, you're making a commitment to yourself to work towards them, which can help you stay on track.

> **Memory:** Writing down your goals can also help you remember them better. When you write something down, you're creating a physical record of it that you can refer back to later. This can be especially helpful if you have a lot of goals or if you're working on a long-term project.

Tracking progress is essential for achieving goals and creating long-term success. It helps to stay motivated, identify areas of improvement, and make necessary adjustments to stay on track. Measuring progress also provides a sense of accomplishment and satisfaction as one sees tangible evidence of their hard work.

Without tracking progress, it is easy to lose motivation or get discouraged, especially if the goal is long-term. Measuring progress allows individuals to see how far they have come and how much closer they are to achieving their goal.

In addition, tracking progress provides valuable insights into the effectiveness of one's actions and strategies. By keeping track of progress, individuals can identify what is working well and what needs to be adjusted to make progress faster or more effectively.

Tracking progress is an essential part of achieving goals. By measuring progress, you can see how far you've come and what still needs to be done. There are different methods for tracking progress, and you should choose the one that works best for you.

One popular method for tracking progress is journaling. You can use a notebook or a digital journal to write down your goals, break them down into smaller steps, and track your progress. Writing down your progress can help you stay motivated and focused.

Another method is to use tracking apps. There are various apps available that can help you track your progress towards your goals. These apps can help you set reminders, track your progress, and visualize your progress over time.

Another effective method is to use an accountability partner. This is someone who can help you stay on track and motivated towards your goals. An accountability partner can be a friend, family member, or even a coach who you check in with regularly to update on your progress and receive feedback.

No matter what method you choose, it's essential to regularly review your progress and adjust your goals and strategies accordingly. Track

Celebrating progress is an important part of the goal-setting process, as it helps to reinforce positive habits and keep motivation high. Here are some tips on how to celebrate progress and stay motivated:

> **Acknowledge your achievements:** Take time to reflect on the progress you've made and acknowledge your achievements, no matter how small they may seem. This will help to build confidence and keep you motivated.

➢ **Reward yourself:** Set up a reward system for reaching milestones or completing specific tasks. This could be something as simple as treating yourself to a favorite snack or indulging in a relaxing activity.

➢ **Share your progress:** Sharing your progress with others can be a great way to stay motivated and accountable. Consider joining a group or finding a friend who can support and encourage you throughout the process.

➢ **Visualize your success:** Take time to visualize yourself achieving your goal and imagine how it will feel when you reach it. This can help to keep you focused and motivated, even during difficult times.

➢ **Stay flexible:** Remember that setbacks and challenges are a normal part of the process. Stay flexible and be willing to adjust your goals and strategies as needed to stay on track.

Common obstacles to goal-setting and tracking progress include:

Lack of motivation can be a common obstacle to goal-setting and tracking progress. It can be challenging to maintain the same level of enthusiasm and commitment for a long period, especially when faced with setbacks or obstacles. Some strategies to overcome a lack of motivation include:

➢ **Revisit your "why":** Remind yourself of the reasons why you set the goal in the first place. What was the motivation behind it? Is it still important to you? Refocusing on your underlying reasons can reignite your motivation.

➢ **Break it down:** Sometimes a goal can feel overwhelming, and this can be demotivating. Breaking the goal down into smaller, achievable steps can help make it feel more manageable and less daunting.

> **Find inspiration:** Seek out inspiration from others who have achieved similar goals or from those who motivate and inspire you. Reading motivational books, listening to inspiring podcasts or attending seminars can help reignite motivation.

> **Adjust the goal:** If the original goal no longer feels motivating or relevant, consider adjusting it. Perhaps you need to change the timeframe, make the goal more specific or relevant, or change the steps required to achieve it.

> **Get support:** Seeking support from friends, family, or a coach can help boost motivation. Accountability partners can help keep you motivated, offer support and guidance when needed, and celebrate your successes with you.

> **Take a break:** Sometimes taking a break can help to recharge motivation. Stepping back and engaging in activities that bring you joy and relaxation can help clear your mind and increase motivation when you return to pursuing your goal.

Fear of failure can be a significant obstacle to achieving goals. It can cause individuals to avoid taking risks and trying new things, which can make it difficult to achieve long-term success. Fear of failure can stem from various factors, including past failures, low self-esteem, and a lack of confidence.

To overcome fear of failure, it is essential to reframe the way you think about failure. Instead of seeing failure as a negative outcome, view it as an opportunity for growth and learning. Recognize that failure is a natural part of the learning process and that every failure can provide valuable insights into how to improve and grow.

Another way to overcome fear of failure is to set realistic goals and focus on progress rather than perfection. Break down your long-term goals into smaller, achievable steps and track your progress along the way. Celebrate small wins and use them as motivation to keep going.

It can also be helpful to seek support from friends, family, or a coach or mentor. Surround yourself with people who believe in you and your goals and who can provide encouragement and guidance when needed. Finally, practice self-compassion and be kind to yourself, recognizing that setbacks and failures are a natural part of the journey towards achieving your goals.

Lack of time is another common obstacle to goal-setting and tracking progress. With busy work schedules, family commitments, and other responsibilities, it can be challenging to find the time to focus on personal goals. However, it's important to remember that setting aside even a small amount of time each day or week can make a significant difference in achieving long-term goals.

One way to overcome this obstacle is to prioritize goal-setting and tracking progress by scheduling time for it in advance. This can mean setting aside time each day, week, or month to review progress and make necessary adjustments. Additionally, finding ways to streamline daily tasks and responsibilities can free up more time to focus on personal goals.

It's also important to recognize that progress towards a goal can be made in small increments, even with limited time. By breaking down long-term goals into smaller, achievable steps and focusing on making progress each day, individuals can stay motivated and achieve success, even with a busy schedule.

One common obstacle to achieving goals and tracking progress is a lack of accountability. When individuals do not have anyone to hold them accountable, they may be less likely to set goals and track their progress. This can make it difficult to stay on track and achieve long-term success.

One solution to this obstacle is to find an accountability partner. An accountability partner can be a friend, family member, or colleague who shares your goals and is committed to helping you achieve them. You can meet regularly to discuss your progress and hold each other accountable for staying on track.

Another solution is to join a support group or community of individuals who are working towards similar goals. This can provide a sense of camaraderie and support, as well as opportunities for accountability.

It's also important to hold yourself accountable by regularly reviewing your goals and progress, and making adjustments as needed. You can do this by setting regular check-ins with yourself, tracking your progress in a journal or app, or using other tracking methods discussed earlier in this chapter.

Ultimately, it's important to remember that achieving your goals is a journey, and setbacks and obstacles are a normal part of the process. By staying accountable and motivated, and making adjustments as needed, you can overcome obstacles and stay on track towards achieving your goals.

Lack of clarity can be a significant obstacle to goal-setting and tracking progress. When goals are vague or undefined, it can be challenging to measure progress and know when the goals have been achieved. This lack of clarity can lead to frustration and a lack of motivation, which can ultimately lead to giving up on the goals.

To overcome this obstacle, it is essential to set clear and specific goals. Instead of setting a goal to "exercise more," for example, set a goal to "exercise for 30 minutes, three times a week." This goal is specific, measurable, and achievable, which makes it easier to track progress and stay motivated.

It is also important to break down larger goals into smaller, more manageable steps. This can help to provide clarity and make it easier to track progress. By breaking down larger goals into smaller steps, individuals can focus on achieving each step and gain a sense of accomplishment along the way.

Regularly revisiting and refining goals can also help to increase clarity. As individuals make progress towards their goals, they may gain new insights or face unexpected challenges. By regularly revisiting and refining goals, individuals can adjust their plans and ensure that they remain focused on achieving their objectives.

Setting unrealistic goals is a common obstacle to achieving success.

When individuals set goals that are too ambitious or difficult to achieve, they may become discouraged and give up on their goals altogether. It is important to set goals that are challenging but achievable. This involves breaking down long-term goals into smaller, manageable steps and setting deadlines for each step. Additionally, it may be helpful to consult with a mentor or expert in the field to gain perspective on what is realistic and achievable. Setting realistic goals can help individuals maintain motivation and stay on track towards achieving their objectives.

Staying motivated and overcoming setbacks is crucial for achieving long-term success in goal-setting and progress tracking. Here are some tips for staying motivated and overcoming setbacks:

> **Focus on the why:** Remember the reasons why you set your goals in the first place. Reconnect with the purpose behind your goals and the benefits you will achieve by reaching them.

> **Break it down:** If you are feeling overwhelmed, break your goals down into smaller, more achievable steps. This can help make your goals feel more manageable and give you a sense of progress as you work towards achieving them.

> **Use positive self-talk:** Practice positive self-talk and use encouraging language when discussing your goals and progress. This can help boost your confidence and keep you motivated.

> **Seek support:** Find a support system that can help hold you accountable and provide encouragement. This can be

friends, family, or a professional coach or mentor.

➤ **Embrace setbacks:** Recognize that setbacks are a natural part of the goal-setting process and use them as an opportunity to learn and grow. Reflect on what went wrong and use that information to adjust your approach and try again.

➤ **Celebrate successes:** Celebrate your successes and milestones along the way, no matter how small they may seem. This can help keep you motivated and provide a sense of accomplishment.

➤ **Stay flexible:** Be willing to adjust your goals and strategies as needed. Life is unpredictable, and sometimes we need to pivot our plans to stay on track towards achieving our goals.

In this chapter, we discussed the importance of setting goals and tracking progress towards achieving them. We highlighted the benefits of setting SMART goals, breaking down long-term goals into smaller achievable steps, and writing down goals to increase accountability. We also explored different methods for tracking progress, including journaling, tracking apps, and accountability partners, and the importance of celebrating progress to stay motivated.

Furthermore, we addressed common obstacles to goal-setting and tracking progress, including lack of motivation, fear of failure, lack of time, lack of accountability, lack of clarity, and setting unrealistic goals. Lastly, we provided tips for staying motivated and overcoming setbacks, such as focusing on the process rather than the outcome, seeking support from others, and learning from mistakes.

By applying these techniques in your own life, you can set yourself up for success and achieve your goals. Remember to stay committed, celebrate progress, and learn from setbacks along the way.

CHAPTER 4: OVERCOMING COMMON OBSTACLES

In order to achieve success, it is important to understand and address the common obstacles that can stand in the way. These obstacles can vary widely, from lack of motivation to fear of failure to time constraints. By identifying and addressing these obstacles, individuals can take steps to overcome them and move closer to achieving their goals. In this chapter, we will explore some of the most common obstacles to success and provide strategies for overcoming them.

Fear of failure is a common obstacle that can hinder an individual's success. This fear can cause individuals to avoid taking risks and trying new things, which can limit their opportunities for growth and development. It can also lead to feelings of anxiety and stress, which can further impede progress towards achieving goals.

One way to overcome the fear of failure is to reframe how failure is perceived. Rather than seeing failure as a negative outcome, individuals can view it as an opportunity to learn and grow. This can help to reduce the fear of failure and encourage individuals to take risks and try new things.

Another way to overcome the fear of failure is to break goals down into smaller, achievable steps. This can help to reduce feelings of overwhelm and increase confidence in one's ability to achieve success. Celebrating small successes along the way can also help to build momentum and increase motivation towards achieving larger goals.

It's also important to have a support system in place. This can include friends, family, or a mentor who can provide encouragement and guidance along the way. Seeking feedback and constructive criticism can also help to reduce the fear of failure by providing a different perspective and helping individuals to improve their skills and performance.

Tips for overcoming the fear of failure include:

> **Reframe failure as a learning opportunity:** Instead of

seeing failure as a negative outcome, try to view it as an opportunity to learn and grow. Each time you fail, ask yourself what you can learn from the experience and how you can apply that knowledge moving forward.

> **Set realistic expectations:** Often, the fear of failure stems from setting unrealistic expectations for ourselves. Instead, try to set realistic and achievable goals. This will help you feel more confident in your ability to succeed and reduce the fear of failure.

> **Focus on progress, not perfection:** Instead of striving for perfection, focus on making progress towards your goals. Celebrate small victories and use them as motivation to keep moving forward.

> **Practice self-compassion:** Be kind to yourself and recognize that everyone makes mistakes. Treat yourself with the same compassion and understanding that you would offer to a friend who is struggling.

> **Take small steps:** Sometimes the fear of failure can be overwhelming, making it difficult to even get started. Break down your goals into smaller, more manageable steps, and focus on taking one step at a time.

By implementing these tips, individuals can learn to overcome their fear of failure and achieve greater success in their personal and professional lives.

Procrastination is a common obstacle that can prevent individuals from achieving their goals. It is the act of delaying or putting off tasks, often until the last minute, and can be a result of various factors, including fear of failure, lack of motivation, or difficulty starting a task.

Procrastination can be detrimental to success because it can lead to missed deadlines, increased stress, and decreased productivity. It can also cause individuals to prioritize short-term gratification over long-term goals.

To overcome procrastination, it is important to identify the root cause and take action to address it. This may involve breaking down tasks into smaller, more manageable steps, setting deadlines, and establishing a routine. It can also be helpful to eliminate distractions, such as social media or other forms of entertainment, while working on tasks.

Additionally, it may be beneficial to reframe the way one thinks about tasks by focusing on the benefits of completing them rather than the negative aspects. Positive self-talk and rewarding oneself for progress can also help to increase motivation and overcome procrastination.

Here are some tips for overcoming procrastination:

➤ **Break tasks into smaller steps:** One of the biggest reasons people procrastinate is because they feel overwhelmed by the size of the task at hand. By breaking a large task into smaller, more manageable steps, it becomes less intimidating and easier to tackle.

➤ **Set deadlines:** Establishing deadlines can be a powerful motivator to overcome procrastination. Set a specific deadline for each step of the task and hold yourself accountable to meeting those deadlines.

➤ **Use a timer:** Set a timer for a certain amount of time and work on the task for that amount of time without any distractions. This technique, called the Pomodoro method, can help you focus and be more productive.

➤ **Create a schedule:** Create a schedule and allocate specific times for working on the task. This can help establish a routine and make it easier to stay on track.

➤ **Eliminate distractions:** Identify and eliminate any

distractions that may be contributing to your procrastination. This could mean turning off your phone or finding a quiet workspace.

> **Get an accountability partner:** Find someone who can hold you accountable for completing the task. This could be a friend, colleague, or mentor who can check in on your progress and provide encouragement.

By using these tips, you can overcome procrastination and achieve your goals more effectively.

Lack of motivation is a common obstacle to achieving success. When individuals lack motivation, they may struggle to take action toward their goals, and may feel stuck or stagnant in their progress. It can be difficult to find the drive and determination to stay focused and committed to long-term goals.

There are several strategies that can be helpful in overcoming a lack of motivation. One effective approach is to identify the underlying reasons for the lack of motivation. Perhaps the goals are not aligned with personal values or interests, or maybe the individual is feeling burnt out and in need of rest and rejuvenation.

Once the root cause of the lack of motivation is identified, it can be helpful to set small, achievable goals that build momentum and provide a sense of accomplishment. Celebrating small wins along the way can help to maintain motivation and momentum.

Another helpful strategy is to find sources of inspiration and support. This could include seeking out a mentor or role model who has achieved similar goals, or joining a support group or community of like-minded individuals.

Finally, it can be helpful to cultivate a growth mindset and focus on the process of achieving goals, rather than solely on the end result. Recognizing that setbacks and challenges are a normal part of the journey can help individuals to maintain motivation and persevere in the face of obstacles.

To increase motivation and overcome a lack of motivation, here are some helpful tips:

1. **Set clear goals** is a crucial factor in increasing motivation and achieving success. When setting goals, it's important to make them specific, measurable, achievable, relevant, and time-bound (SMART). This helps to ensure that the goals are clear and achievable, which can boost motivation.

   To set clear goals, start by identifying what you want to achieve. Make sure that the goals are specific and well-defined. For example, instead of setting a goal to "get in shape," set a goal to "lose 10 pounds in three months by exercising three times a week and following a healthy diet."
   Next, make sure that your goals are measurable. This means that you should be able to track your progress and see how far you've come. For example, you might track your weight loss progress by weighing yourself once a week and keeping a log.

   Ensure that your goals are achievable. It's important to set goals that challenge you, but not ones that are so difficult that you become discouraged. Be realistic about what you can achieve within a given time frame.

   Make sure that your goals are relevant to your overall vision for your life. Ask yourself why you want to achieve these goals and how they fit into your larger aspirations.

   Finally, set a specific time frame for achieving your goals. This helps to create a sense of urgency and can increase motivation. For example, you might set a goal to lose 10 pounds in three months.

   By setting clear and achievable goals, you can boost your motivation and increase your chances of success.

2. **Break down goals into smaller tasks:** Breaking down larger goals into smaller, manageable tasks is a great way to increase motivation and prevent procrastination. When a goal feels too big or complex, it can be challenging to know where to start or to feel like progress is being made. By breaking it down into smaller tasks, you can create a clear roadmap to follow and build momentum as you complete each step.

To break down your goals into smaller tasks, start by identifying the key milestones or components of your goal. Then, break these down into smaller tasks that you can realistically achieve in a shorter period of time, such as a day or a week. Try to create tasks that are specific and actionable, so that you know exactly what needs to be done.

For example, if your goal is to write a book, you might break it down into tasks such as:

✓ Research and outline chapter 1

✓ Write 500 words of chapter 1

✓ Revise and edit chapter 1

✓ Research and outline chapter 2

✓ Write 500 words of chapter 2

✓ And so on...

By breaking your goal into smaller tasks, you can see the progress you're making and feel motivated to keep going. Plus, completing each task gives you a sense of accomplishment, which can further boost your motivation.

3. **Create a plan:** Creating a plan can be an effective way to increase motivation and overcome obstacles. By outlining the specific steps you need to take to achieve your goals, you can create a roadmap for success. A plan can provide structure and direction, which can help to reduce feelings of overwhelm and increase motivation.

   When creating a plan, it's important to be specific and break down your goals into smaller, actionable steps. Identify the key milestones or deadlines you need to meet, and then plan out the tasks required to achieve those milestones. Be sure to include realistic timelines and take into account any potential obstacles or challenges that may arise.

   Having a plan can also help to hold you accountable. You can track your progress against the plan and adjust as needed to stay on track. Additionally, seeing the progress you're making towards your goals can be a powerful motivator.

   There are many tools and techniques that can help you create and stick to a plan. For example, you can use a project management tool or a planner to track your progress and stay organized. You can also use visualization techniques to imagine yourself achieving your goals and visualize the steps you need to take to get there.

4. **Focus on the benefits:** When you're feeling unmotivated, remind yourself of the benefits of achieving your goals. This can help to reinvigorate your drive and increase your desire to succeed.

   Focusing on the benefits of achieving your goals can be a powerful motivator. Consider the positive impact that achieving your goals can have on your life, such as increased happiness, financial stability, or personal growth. When you feel unmotivated, take a moment to reflect on these benefits and how achieving your goals can improve your life. You can even create a vision board or list of the benefits to refer to when you need a boost of motivation. By keeping your eye on the prize, you can stay motivated and focused on achieving your goals.

5. **Visualizing success** is an effective technique for increasing motivation and overcoming obstacles. By imagining yourself achieving your goals, you can create a mental picture of what success looks like and how it will feel. This can help to create a sense of excitement and anticipation, which can fuel your motivation and drive you towards your goals.

   To visualize success, start by finding a quiet, comfortable place where you won't be interrupted. Close your eyes and imagine yourself achieving your goals. See yourself completing the tasks you need to do, and enjoying the benefits that come with success. Imagine how it will feel to have accomplished what you set out to do, and how it will impact your life in a positive way.

   As you visualize success, try to engage all your senses. Imagine what you'll see, hear, and feel as you achieve your goals. This will help to create a more vivid and realistic picture in your mind, which can make it easier to stay motivated and focused.

   Visualization is a technique used by many successful individuals, including athletes and business leaders. It can help you to overcome self-doubt and increase your confidence in your ability to achieve your goals. With regular practice, visualization can become a powerful tool for staying motivated and overcoming obstacles on your path to success.

6. **Getting support** from others is an effective way to increase motivation and overcome obstacles. When you have people in your life who believe in you and support your goals, it can make a significant difference in your ability to stay motivated and keep moving forward.

Here are some ways to get support:

✓ **Share your goals with others:** Letting others know about your goals can help to hold you accountable and provide support when you need it. You can share your goals with friends, family, or even a coach or mentor.

✓ **Join a group:** Joining a group of like-minded individuals who are working towards similar goals can provide a sense of community and support. You can find groups online or in-person.

✓ **Hire a coach:** A coach can provide personalized support and guidance to help you overcome obstacles and achieve your goals.

✓ **Find a workout partner:** If your goal is related to fitness or health, finding a workout partner can provide motivation and support.

✓ **Attend events and workshops:** Attend events and workshops related to your goals. This can help to keep you motivated and provide opportunities to learn from others who have achieved similar goals.

Remember, getting support from others is not a sign of weakness. It's a sign of strength and a recognition that achieving goals can be challenging and that it's okay to ask for help.

7. **Celebrate progress:** It's important to acknowledge and celebrate the progress you make towards your goals, no matter how small it may be. Celebrating progress can provide a sense of accomplishment and increase motivation. It can also help to build momentum towards achieving your ultimate goal. Set up milestones along the way and reward yourself for achieving them. This can be as simple as treating yourself to your favorite snack or

taking a day off to relax. By celebrating your progress, you're reminding yourself of the progress you've made and encouraging yourself to keep moving forward.

Perfectionism can be a major obstacle to achieving success as it can lead to self-criticism, procrastination, and an inability to take risks. The constant need to achieve perfection can also lead to burnout and a lack of satisfaction with accomplishments.

People who struggle with perfectionism often have unrealistic expectations for themselves and fear failure or making mistakes. This fear can paralyze them from taking action, even if it means missing out on opportunities for growth and success.

It's important to recognize that perfectionism is not a healthy or sustainable approach to achieving success. Instead, focusing on progress and growth can lead to more sustainable and fulfilling outcomes.

Overcoming perfectionism can be a challenging but important step towards achieving success. Here are some tips that can help:

> **Accept imperfection:** Understand that nobody is perfect and that it's okay to make mistakes. Perfectionism can lead to feelings of shame and self-criticism, which can be detrimental to motivation and progress. Embrace imperfection as a part of the learning process and allow yourself to make mistakes.

> **Focus on progress, not perfection:** Rather than striving for perfection, focus on making progress towards your goals. Celebrate small wins and milestones along the way, and recognize that progress, even if it's not perfect, is still progress.

> **Set realistic expectations:** Set goals and expectations that are realistic and achievable. Unrealistic expectations can lead to feelings of failure and inadequacy, which can fuel perfectionism. By setting realistic expectations, you

can work towards achieving your goals without the pressure of perfectionism.

➤ **Practice self-compassion:** Be kind to yourself and practice self-compassion. Treat yourself with the same kindness and understanding that you would offer to a friend who is struggling. Self-criticism and harsh self-judgment can fuel perfectionism and hinder progress.

➤ **Embrace mistakes as opportunities for growth:** Rather than viewing mistakes as failures, see them as opportunities for growth and learning. Embracing mistakes can help you to develop resilience and a growth mindset, which can be valuable assets in achieving success.

Remember, perfectionism can be a significant obstacle to achieving success. By accepting imperfection, focusing on progress, setting realistic expectations, practicing self-compassion, and embracing mistakes, you can overcome perfectionism and work towards achieving your goals.

Distractions can have a significant impact on productivity and success. With the increasing prevalence of technology, distractions can come in many forms, such as social media notifications, email alerts, or even background noise. Distractions can lead to a lack of focus, procrastination, and a decrease in productivity, making it challenging to achieve goals and meet deadlines.

In addition, distractions can also lead to a decrease in the quality of work. When individuals are distracted, they may not be giving their full attention to the task at hand, resulting in errors or omissions that can have a negative impact on success.

It is important to identify the sources of distraction and take steps to minimize their impact. This can include turning off notifications, setting designated times for checking email or social media, or finding a quiet space to work without distractions. By reducing distractions, individuals can increase their focus and productivity, allowing them to achieve their goals more efficiently and effectively.

There are several tips that can help minimize distractions and increase productivity:

➢ **Create a designated workspace:** Having a specific place where you work can help to minimize distractions and increase focus. Ideally, this workspace should be free of clutter and other distractions.

➢ **Turn off notifications:** Notifications from social media, email, and other apps can be major distractions. Consider turning off notifications or scheduling times to check them throughout the day.

➢ **Use time blocking:** Time blocking involves scheduling specific blocks of time for different tasks. This can help to increase productivity by providing structure and minimizing distractions.

➢ **Prioritize tasks:** Prioritizing tasks based on their importance can help you stay focused on what's most important and minimize distractions from less important tasks.

➢ **Take breaks:** Taking breaks can actually help to increase productivity by providing time to recharge and refocus. Consider taking short breaks every hour or so to stretch or take a quick walk.

A lack of time can be a significant obstacle to achieving goals. Many people struggle to find time to focus on their goals due to busy work schedules or other personal commitments. When individuals feel overwhelmed and unable to prioritize their time, they may become discouraged and lose sight of their goals.

One way to overcome this obstacle is to create a schedule or routine that prioritizes time for goal-setting and progress tracking. This may involve making small changes to daily habits or delegating tasks to free up more time. Additionally, it can be helpful to break down goals into smaller tasks that can be accomplished in shorter periods of time.

Another approach is to reassess priorities and determine which goals are most important. This may involve making difficult decisions about how to allocate time and resources. By focusing on the most important goals and letting go of less important ones, individuals can ensure that they are making the most of their limited time.

Ultimately, overcoming a lack of time requires a combination of prioritization, organization, and discipline. By taking a proactive approach to managing time, individuals can make progress towards their goals and achieve success despite the constraints of a busy schedule.

Here are some tips for managing time effectively:

➢ **Prioritize tasks:** Make a list of tasks in order of importance and focus on completing the most important ones first.

➢ **Set realistic deadlines:** Be realistic when setting deadlines for yourself and take into account unexpected events that may delay progress.

➢ **Delegate responsibilities:** If possible, delegate tasks to others who may be able to complete them more efficiently or have more expertise in the area.

➢ **Use time management tools:** Consider using tools such as calendars, to-do lists, and time tracking apps to help manage your time more effectively.

➢ **Minimize distractions:** As discussed earlier, minimize distractions by creating a designated workspace and turning off notifications on your phone or computer.

➢ **Take breaks:** Taking regular breaks can help to increase productivity and prevent burnout. Be sure to schedule in time for breaks throughout your day.

➢ **Learn to say no:** It's important to learn to say no to requests that may distract you from your priorities or overload your schedule.

By implementing these tips, you can manage your time more effectively and make progress towards achieving your goals.

In conclusion, there are several common obstacles that can hinder progress and success, including fear of failure, procrastination, lack of motivation, perfectionism, distractions, and lack of time. By recognizing these obstacles and implementing strategies to overcome them, individuals can increase their chances of achieving their goals. Strategies such as reframing failure, breaking down goals into smaller tasks, setting clear goals, visualizing success, seeking support, minimizing distractions, and managing time effectively can all help individuals overcome common obstacles and achieve success. It is important to remember that progress takes time and setbacks are a natural part of the process. With persistence and determination, anyone can overcome obstacles and achieve their goals.

CHAPTER 5: MINDSET SHIFTS FOR LASTING CHANGE

Mindset plays a significant role in our ability to achieve lasting change. Our mindset is our attitude or perception towards our abilities, potential, and circumstances. When we have a growth mindset, we believe that our abilities and intelligence can be developed through hard work and dedication. On the other hand, a fixed mindset is a belief that our abilities are fixed and cannot be changed. By shifting our mindset, we can change our behaviors, habits, and actions, leading to lasting change. In this chapter, we'll explore some of the key mindset shifts that can help us achieve long-term success.

Having the right mindset is essential in achieving lasting change. There are two main mindsets that people typically have: a fixed mindset and a growth mindset.

A fixed mindset is a belief that abilities, intelligence, and traits are inherent and unchangeable. People with a fixed mindset often avoid challenges and give up easily when faced with obstacles, believing that their abilities are limited and cannot be improved.

On the other hand, a growth mindset is a belief that abilities, intelligence, and traits can be developed and improved through hard work and dedication. People with a growth mindset embrace challenges and persist through obstacles, believing that their abilities can be developed and strengthened over time.

Having a growth mindset can lead to greater resilience, creativity, and motivation, as individuals are more likely to take risks, learn from mistakes, and embrace new opportunities for growth and development.

A fixed mindset refers to a belief that one's abilities, talents, and intelligence are predetermined and cannot be changed. Those with a fixed mindset tend to avoid challenges and view failure as a reflection of their innate abilities. They may also be resistant to feedback and view it as a threat to their sense of self. People with a fixed mindset may also compare themselves to others, often feeling either superior or inferior based on their perceived innate abilities. This can lead to a fear of taking risks and reluctance to try new things.

A fixed mindset can hinder personal growth and achievement in several ways. Firstly, individuals with a fixed mindset often believe that their abilities are set in stone and cannot be developed or improved upon. As a result, they may avoid challenges or opportunities that could help them grow and develop their skills. They may also become defensive or disheartened when faced with criticism or setbacks because they view these as an indication of their innate limitations.

Furthermore, a fixed mindset can lead to a fear of failure and a reluctance to take risks. Individuals with a fixed mindset may believe that failure is a sign of weakness or incompetence, rather than an opportunity to learn and improve. This can cause them to avoid taking on new challenges or pursuing their goals, limiting their potential for growth and success.

A growth mindset is the belief that personal qualities, such as intelligence and ability, can be developed through effort and hard work. It is the opposite of a fixed mindset, which is the belief that these qualities are fixed and cannot be changed.

People with a growth mindset embrace challenges and view failures as opportunities to learn and grow. They are willing to take risks, seek out new experiences, and put in the effort required to achieve their goals. They also believe that their abilities can be improved through practice and perseverance.

Individuals with a growth mindset are more likely to have a positive attitude towards personal growth and achievement, and are more resilient in the face of setbacks and challenges. They see challenges as opportunities to learn and grow, rather than as threats to their abilities or self-worth.

A growth mindset is a belief that one's abilities and intelligence can be developed through hard work, dedication, and learning. Individuals with a growth mindset tend to see challenges as opportunities for growth and are more likely to persevere through obstacles. They embrace mistakes as learning opportunities and view failures as setbacks to be overcome rather than reasons to give up. Those with a growth mindset tend to be more resilient and adaptable, and are more likely to achieve their goals in the long run.

A growth mindset allows individuals to see themselves as constantly evolving, and to believe that they can always improve and develop their skills and knowledge. This belief system enables people to take risks, learn from their mistakes, and ultimately achieve greater success in their personal and professional lives. By adopting a growth mindset, individuals are more likely to develop a love of learning, and to enjoy the process of working towards their goals, rather than solely focusing on the end result.

Having a growth mindset is crucial for achieving lasting change because it allows you to embrace challenges and view failures as opportunities for growth. Here are some tips for shifting from a fixed mindset to a growth mindset:

> **Embrace challenges:** Instead of shying away from challenges, embrace them as opportunities to learn and grow. Recognize that challenges are necessary for personal growth and development.

> **View failure as a learning opportunity:** Instead of viewing failure as a sign of weakness, view it as an opportunity to learn and improve. Failure is a natural part of the learning process, and it can provide valuable insights for future success.

> **Practice self-compassion:** Treat yourself with kindness and compassion, especially when facing setbacks or challenges. Recognize that mistakes and failures are part of the human experience, and use them as opportunities for growth rather than self-criticism.

> **Cultivate a growth mindset environment:** Surround yourself with people who support and encourage a growth

mindset. Avoid those who reinforce a fixed mindset or discourage personal growth.

➤ **Focus on the process:** Instead of solely focusing on the end result, focus on the process of learning and growth. Embrace the journey, celebrate progress, and learn from challenges along the way.

By shifting to a growth mindset, you can achieve lasting change and reach your full potential.

Here are some tips for shifting from a fixed mindset to a growth mindset:

➤ **Embrace challenges:** Instead of avoiding challenges and sticking to what you already know, embrace new challenges as opportunities for growth and learning.

➤ **Learn from mistakes:** Rather than viewing mistakes as failures, see them as opportunities to learn and improve. Analyze your mistakes and figure out how you can do better next time.

➤ **Practice self-awareness:** Be mindful of your thoughts and reactions to situations. Notice when you're thinking in a fixed mindset and challenge those thoughts to adopt a growth mindset.

➤ **Use positive self-talk:** Focus on your strengths and use positive self-talk to boost your confidence and motivation. Encourage yourself to keep going and remind yourself that you're capable of learning and growing.

➤ **Surround yourself with growth-minded people:** Seek out people who have a growth mindset and who can support and encourage your personal growth.

➤ **Emphasize effort over natural ability:** Instead of believing that you either have natural talent or you don't, focus on the effort you put into achieving your goals. Recognize that hard work and persistence can lead to success.

➢ **Embrace learning and growth:** Cultivate a love for learning and see it as a lifelong journey rather than a destination. Embrace new experiences and seek out opportunities to learn and grow.

In conclusion, mindset plays a critical role in achieving lasting change. A fixed mindset can hinder personal growth and achievement, while a growth mindset can facilitate it. Shifting from a fixed mindset to a growth mindset is possible, and it involves embracing challenges, learning from mistakes, and focusing on effort and improvement rather than just innate ability. By adopting a growth mindset, individuals can develop new skills, achieve their goals, and overcome obstacles in their personal and professional lives. Therefore, it's important to recognize the power of mindset and take steps to shift towards a growth mindset to achieve lasting change.

CHAPTER 6: CASE STUDIES AND SUCCESS STORIES

Case studies and success stories provide valuable insights into the strategies and techniques used by individuals and organizations to achieve their goals. By examining the experiences of others, we can learn from their successes and failures and apply those lessons to our own lives and endeavors.

In this chapter, we will explore the stories of several individuals and organizations who have achieved remarkable success in various fields. We will examine the mindset shifts, strategies, and techniques that they used to overcome obstacles and achieve their goals. Through these stories, we can gain inspiration and valuable insights into how we too can achieve our own goals and aspirations.

The individuals and organizations featured in this chapter include:

- ✓ **Elon Musk:** founder of SpaceX, Tesla, and other successful companies

- ✓ **Oprah Winfrey:** media mogul and philanthropist

- ✓ **Mahatma Gandhi:** Indian independence leader and advocate of nonviolent resistance

- ✓ **Apple Inc.:** technology company known for innovative products and design

- ✓ **Nelson Mandela:** anti-apartheid revolutionary and former president of South Africa

Each of these individuals and organizations has achieved remarkable success through their unique approaches and strategies, which we will explore in detail in the following sections.

Elon Musk is a South African-born entrepreneur and innovator who is known for his ambitious and groundbreaking projects in the technology, transportation, and space industries. Musk is the founder of several successful companies, including SpaceX, Tesla, Neuralink, and The Boring Company.

Musk's approach to entrepreneurship is characterized by a growth mindset and a relentless pursuit of his goals. He is known for his willingness to take risks, embrace failure, and learn from his mistakes. Musk is also highly focused and has a clear vision for the future, which he pursues with unwavering determination.

Musk's strategies for achieving success are multifaceted and include a strong focus on innovation, collaboration, and disruption. He is known for his unconventional ideas and his willingness to challenge the status quo. Musk's companies are also highly focused on sustainability and reducing humanity's impact on the environment.

Through his innovative and ambitious projects, Elon Musk has demonstrated that success is achievable through a combination of hard work, determination, and a willingness to take risks and pursue unconventional ideas.

Oprah Winfrey is an American media mogul, philanthropist, and former talk show host who is known for her influential and empowering messages. Winfrey began her career in broadcasting in the 1970s and rose to national prominence with her daytime talk show, The Oprah Winfrey Show, which aired from 1986 to 2011.

Winfrey's approach to media and philanthropy is characterized by a growth mindset and a focus on personal empowerment and social change. She is known for her emphasis on authenticity, vulnerability, and empathy, and for her ability to connect with and inspire her audience.

Winfrey's strategies for building a successful media empire include a strong focus on storytelling, collaboration, and diversification. She has also been highly innovative in her use of technology and social media to connect with her audience and promote her brand. Additionally, Winfrey is deeply committed to philanthropy, particularly in the areas of education and social justice.

Through her groundbreaking work in media and philanth

Mahatma Gandhi was an Indian independence leader who fought for India's independence from British colonial rule. He was born in 1869 in Porbandar, India, and was educated in law in England. After returning to India, Gandhi became an advocate for Indian rights and worked towards achieving Indian independence through nonviolent resistance.

Gandhi's philosophy of nonviolent resistance, also known as Satyagraha, was inspired by his beliefs in truth and morality. He believed that peaceful protest and civil disobedience could be used to challenge oppressive systems and effect change. Throughout his life, Gandhi led numerous campaigns, including the Salt March and the Quit India movement, which contributed to India's eventual independence in 1947.

In addition to his political activism, Gandhi was also a proponent of self-improvement and personal growth. He encouraged individuals to examine their own lives and behaviors and make changes to promote their own growth and the growth of their communities.

Gandhi's legacy continues to inspire individuals and movements around the world. His philosophy of nonviolent resistance has been used by countless individuals and organizations in their efforts to effect change and promote social justice.

Apple Inc. is a technology company that is widely recognized for its innovative products, cutting-edge design, and sophisticated marketing strategies. Founded in 1976 by Steve Jobs, Steve Wozniak, and Ronald Wayne, the company has revolutionized the personal computer, smartphone, and music industries, among others.

One of Apple's biggest success stories is the introduction of the iPhone in 2007. The iPhone's touchscreen interface, intuitive user experience, and sleek design made it an instant hit with consumers, and it quickly became the company's flagship product. The iPhone's success has continued to fuel Apple's growth, with the company selling over 2.2 billion iPhones as of 2021.

Apple's commitment to innovation and design excellence has also helped it to create a brand that is synonymous with quality and luxury. The company's products are known for their distinctive design aesthetic, use of premium materials, and attention to detail. This has allowed Apple to charge a premium for its products, resulting in high profit margins and a loyal customer base.

In addition to its focus on product innovation, Apple has also been successful in its marketing efforts. The company's "Think Different" campaign in the late 1990s and early 2000s, which featured iconic figures such as Mahatma Gandhi and Albert Einstein, helped to position Apple as a leader in the technology industry and solidify its brand identity.

Overall, Apple's success can be attributed to its focus on innovation, design excellence, and effective marketing strategies. By consistently delivering products that exceed customer expectations and creating a strong brand identity, Apple has been able to maintain its position as one of the world's most valuable companies.

Nelson Mandela was a South African anti-apartheid revolutionary and politician who served as the country's first black president from 1994 to 1999. He is widely regarded as one of the most important figures in modern history for his role in ending apartheid and promoting racial reconciliation in South Africa.

Mandela was born in 1918 in the Eastern Cape province of South Africa. He became involved in anti-apartheid activism as a young man and joined the African National Congress (ANC) in the 1940s. In 1962, he was arrested and sentenced to life in prison for his role in the ANC's sabotage campaign against the government.

Mandela spent 27 years in prison, during which time he became a symbol of the anti-apartheid movement and a global icon for freedom and human rights. He was released in 1990 and played a leading role in negotiations with the government that led to the end of apartheid and the establishment of a democratic government in 1994.

As president, Mandela worked to heal the deep racial divisions in

South African society and promote reconciliation between black and white South Africans. He oversaw the creation of a new constitution and the establishment of the Truth and Reconciliation Commission, which investigated human rights abuses committed during the apartheid era.

Mandela was widely admired for his humility, integrity, and commitment to justice and equality. He was awarded the Nobel Peace Prize in 1993 for his work in promoting peaceful resolution of conflicts and advancing human rights.

Mandela's legacy continues to inspire people around the world to work for social justice and equality. His life and work serve as a powerful reminder of the importance of perseverance, courage, and compassion in the face of oppression and injustice.

CHAPTER 7: THE FUTURE OF HABIT FORMATION

Habit formation is critical for personal and professional success because it helps individuals to establish routines and behaviors that support their goals. By forming positive habits, individuals can automate their actions and reduce the cognitive load associated with decision-making, allowing them to focus on higher-level tasks and achieve greater productivity. Furthermore, habits can help to promote overall health and well-being, as consistent behaviors can lead to improved physical and mental health outcomes. In this chapter, we will explore the future of habit formation and the emerging trends and technologies that are changing the way we approach this important aspect of personal development.

Technology has the potential to revolutionize habit formation by providing new and innovative ways to track and reinforce positive behaviors. Wearable devices such as fitness trackers and smartwatches can track physical activity, sleep patterns, and other health metrics, providing real-time feedback to users and encouraging them to meet daily goals. Mobile apps and online platforms can also be used to track progress, set reminders, and provide support and motivation. For example, there are apps that help users form habits by setting up daily reminders, offering rewards, and providing personalized coaching. The use of technology in habit formation can also provide valuable data for researchers and healthcare professionals, allowing them to gain insights into the most effective methods for habit formation and behavior change. As technology continues to advance, the potential for using it to facilitate habit formation is only likely to grow.

In recent years, there has been an increasing interest in using technology to facilitate habit formation. From fitness trackers to habit tracking apps and virtual assistants, various technologies have been developed to help people develop and maintain good habits.

Fitness trackers, such as Fitbit and Garmin, are designed to monitor physical activity and provide feedback on progress. They can help individuals set and achieve fitness goals by providing data on steps taken, calories burned, and other metrics. By setting goals and tracking progress, users can develop healthy exercise habits and maintain motivation.

Habit tracking apps, such as Habitica and Streaks, are designed to help individuals track and develop good habits. Users can set up daily or weekly habits they want to establish, and the app will remind them to complete them. The apps can track progress over time and provide motivation through rewards or gamification.

Virtual assistants, such as Amazon's Alexa and Google Assistant, can also be used to facilitate habit formation. Users can set reminders, create to-do lists, and receive daily inspirational messages. By integrating habit formation into their daily routines, individuals can develop and maintain good habits.

While technology can be a useful tool in habit formation, it is important to note that it is not a magic solution. Ultimately, it is up to the individual to commit to developing and maintaining good habits. Technology can provide support and motivation, but it is not a substitute for personal responsibility and commitment to change.

While technology can be a powerful tool to aid in habit formation, it also has potential drawbacks that should be considered.

One benefit of technology is that it can provide a convenient and accessible way to track habits and progress. Fitness trackers and habit tracking apps, for example, can provide valuable data and insights that can help individuals make more informed decisions about their habits. Virtual assistants and reminders can also serve as helpful prompts to encourage habit formation.

However, relying too heavily on technology for habit formation can also have drawbacks. For example, it can lead to a sense of dependence on the technology, and individuals may struggle to maintain habits without the assistance of the technology. Additionally, some individuals may become overly focused on achieving certain metrics or goals, which can lead to a fixation on numbers rather than the overall benefits of the habit.

It is important to approach technology as a tool to assist in habit formation, rather than a replacement for personal responsibility and accountability. It is also important to remember that while technology can provide useful information and reminders, it cannot replace the hard work and dedication required to form lasting habits.

Habit formation is a complex process that involves various neural processes. When a behavior is repeated regularly, it becomes automatic and is stored in the basal ganglia, a brain region involved in the formation and retrieval of habitual behaviors. This process involves the reinforcement of neural connections between the basal ganglia and the prefrontal cortex, a region involved in decision-making and self-control. As the behavior becomes more habitual, the prefrontal cortex is less involved in the decision-making process, and the behavior is triggered automatically in response to specific cues or stimuli. This is why breaking a habit can be difficult, as it involves rewiring these neural connections.

Research in neuroscience has shown that there are several neurotransmitters involved in habit formation, including dopamine, a chemical that is released in response to pleasurable experiences and helps to reinforce habitual behaviors. Other neurotransmitters, such as serotonin and noradrenaline, are involved in regulating mood and motivation and can influence the formation of habits. Understanding the neural processes involved in habit formation can help individuals to develop strategies for breaking bad habits and forming new, healthier ones.

Recent neuroscience research has shed light on the neural processes involved in habit formation, providing insight into how habits can be effectively formed and changed. Studies have shown that habits are formed through the repetition of behavior, which leads to the strengthening of neural connections in the brain. As habits become more automatic, they are controlled by a different part of the brain than intentional actions.

One important finding is that habits can be disrupted and changed by introducing new experiences and learning opportunities. This suggests that creating new experiences or adding variety to daily routines may be an effective way to break old habits and form new ones.

Another interesting finding is that the timing and context of habits can have a significant impact on their formation and change. For example, habits formed in response to specific cues or triggers may be more difficult to change if those cues are still present in the environment. On the other hand, habits formed in response to positive reinforcement may be more easily changed if alternative sources of reinforcement are introduced.

Cultural and social factors can have a significant impact on habit formation. These factors include societal norms, peer pressure, family expectations, and cultural traditions. For example, in some cultures, it may be customary to eat large, heavy meals late in the evening, which can contribute to unhealthy eating habits. Similarly, peer pressure can influence individuals to engage in unhealthy habits, such as smoking or excessive drinking.

On the other hand, cultural and social factors can also facilitate healthy habit formation. For instance, in cultures that prioritize physical activity and outdoor recreation, individuals may be more likely to develop habits that involve regular exercise and outdoor activity. Additionally, social support from family, friends, and communities can be a powerful motivator for individuals to adopt and maintain healthy habits.

It is important to recognize the influence of cultural and social factors on habit formation and to identify ways to leverage these factors to support healthy behavior change. This may involve seeking out social support from peers or joining groups that promote healthy habits, as well as challenging societal norms or cultural practices that may contribute to unhealthy behaviors.

Leveraging cultural and social influences can be a powerful way to support habit formation. One way to do this is to find a community of people who share your goals and habits. This can provide social support and accountability, making it easier to stick to your habits. For example, if you are trying to develop a regular exercise routine, joining a fitness class or workout group can help you stay motivated and committed.

Another way to leverage cultural and social influences is to make the desired behavior part of your identity. This can involve adopting a new cultural or social identity that is aligned with the habit you are trying to form. For example, if you want to eat a healthier diet, you could start identifying as a "health-conscious" person and surround yourself with others who share this identity.

Finally, it is important to recognize that cultural and social influences can also create barriers to habit formation. For example, if your cultural or social group values a behavior that is incompatible with your desired habit, it may be harder to stick to it. In these cases, it may be helpful to seek out a new community or to find ways to shift the cultural or social norms to better support your habit-forming efforts.

In conclusion, habit formation is a crucial aspect of personal and professional success. With the potential of technology to facilitate habit formation, it is important to recognize the benefits and drawbacks of relying on technology to develop and maintain positive habits. Additionally, recent neuroscience research has provided insights into the neural processes involved in habit formation, which can help to develop effective habit formation techniques. Cultural and social influences also play a significant role in habit formation, and leveraging these influences can support the development of positive habits. By prioritizing habit formation and utilizing various techniques and resources, individuals can improve their chances of achieving long-term success.

CHAPTER 8: CONCLUSION AND ACTION STEPS

In conclusion, developing automatic habits is crucial for achieving personal and professional success. The key to habit formation is consistency and repetition over time, and there are several strategies and techniques that can be used to develop and maintain positive habits.

Some of the key takeaways from this book include understanding the habit loop, setting clear goals and intentions, identifying and addressing obstacles to habit formation, and adopting a growth mindset. Additionally, leveraging technology and social support can be effective in facilitating habit formation.

To take action towards developing automatic habits, consider the following steps:

➢ Identify the habits you want to develop and why they are important to you.

➢ Use the habit loop to break down the habit into specific cues, routines, and rewards.

➢ Set clear goals and intentions for each habit, and track your progress using a habit tracking app or journal.

➢ Anticipate and address potential obstacles to habit formation, such as lack of motivation or distractions.

➢ Practice self-compassion and embrace mistakes and setbacks as opportunities for growth.

➢ Leverage technology and social support to reinforce positive habits.

➢ Celebrate progress and acknowledge achievements, no matter how small.

By consistently applying these strategies and techniques, you can develop automatic habits that support your personal and professional goals and lead to lasting change.

ABOUT THE AUTHOR

Thank you for reading book.